Insurance Billing

For

CAM Providers

A Survival Guide For
Alternative Medicine Practitioners

John C. Donald, L.Ac.

Samsara Publishing

Samsara Publishing
5825 -221st Place SE, Suite 204
Issaquah, WA 98027

Receive Continuing Education Credits For Reading This Book

If you are interested in receiving continuing education credit for learning what is contained in this book please visit our website to take an online quiz after you have completed reading the book. For a very reasonable fee you may receive professional CEU's that may be applied toward professional re-certification.

Billing Forms Available On CDrom

If you would like to have a great resource for billing forms as well as charts and templates referenced in this book please visit our website where you can purchase an optional, companion CDrom containing many templates in Word format which you can edit to include your own practice information.

Visit Us At:

www.SamsaraPublishing.com

Table Of Contents

Introduction

When I began my acupuncture training in 1995 most CAM practitioners in my area were maintaining cozy little cash practices, with many working out of their homes. It was the essence of a true cottage industry that reflected the mellow and laid-back approach that many of these people took to their lives.

By the time I graduated and hung out my shingle there was a new state mandate that insurance plans were to include CAM benefits and the landscape had changed significantly. This proved to be a mixed blessing. While it has made CAM more accessible to patients, it also made life more stressful for providers. Practitioners were rapidly being herded into panels of "preferred providers" for the various insurance plans and were signing contracts pushed upon them to accept reduced fees and increased administrative duties.

No longer could practitioners work out of their home if they wanted to be a "preferred provider. They also had to take on the extra expenses of maintaining malpractice and liability insurance and needed to invest money and time into managing complicated systems of accounts receivables.

Like it or not, complimentary and alternative medicine has been assimilated into the dominant paradigm of the insurance industry. Many practitioners who used to complain about the lack of insurance coverage for CAM services now lament the myriad of frustrating rules and often frequent rule changes that apply to the increasingly available coverage.

It is apparent that very few CAM providers have taken the time to educate themselves about this significant and important part of their practice. Most of the practitioners I talk to who describe ongoing patterns of frustrating experiences simply misunderstand how the insurance industry works and they have unrealistic expectations of this very impersonal industry.

Counter to appearances, the insurance companies are not in business to pay claims. They are in business to charge premiums from their members. They profit from keeping their expenses as low as possible just like you do. You are one of their expenses.

This modern-day David & Goliath dynamic can be made easier to digest, however, by taking the time to really understand how the insurance reimbursement system works and how to participate in it in a way that won't deplete your resources. It is important to remember that we create our own reality. As business owners we must plot our own course and make decisions that are financially responsible. If participating in the insurance reimbursement scheme furthers the goals of your business then you owe it to yourself to create a clear system for managing all of the details that come with this territory.

This book will discuss the fundamental principles of insurance billing and reimbursement and give you specific tools to successfully negotiate the relationship between provider and payer.

In an ideal world we would be paid fairly and promptly for services rendered and stay busy enough to flourish and thrive. For some, it makes sense to stay with a cash practice model if that is working for them. For others it seems that unless they begin processing claims on behalf of their patients they will lose business to the next practitioner down the street who is already doing it.

This fear-based tactic is commonly employed by insurers in order to convince a practitioner to sign on as a "preferred provider". They say "if you don't sign up with us then your competitors will and there will be no patients left for you". However, if you look around you will find practitioners in every town with successful, cash-only practices. Most of them have taken several years to build up to this point but if you have the luxury of time and resources on your side then why bother to get involved in the hoopla?

Look at it from different angles and see what might motivate you to play this insurance billing game. If you are new in business and are struggling for patients then signing a contract to become a "preferred provider" will theoretically drive more patients to your practice. Perhaps you have chosen to locate your practice in an area where there are numerous other practitioners and you are looking for a unique advantage. Providing billing services for your patients is a convenience for them and may provide you with a competitive edge.

In most geographic regions a majority of patients have health insurance. If their insurance policies include coverage for CAM services most patients will seek out a practitioner who is willing to bill their insurance versus paying full-fare for a non-participating practitioner. This is just human nature.

Obviously it is the desire of all practitioners to have a bustling practice that thrives solely through word-of-mouth referrals and many eventually do accomplish this through diligent practice building and providing effective care over time. It is very frustrating, however, to have a prospective patient referred to you only to have them go elsewhere because you cannot bill their insurance plan.

Many patients simply cannot afford to pay out of pocket and if no practitioners are willing to bill insurance on the patient's behalf they won't be able to utilize CAM services. Seen in this light, you could be providing a significant service to those in your community who would otherwise find your medicine inaccessible by offering to process claims for them.

New practices get busy faster when there are fewer obstacles to the patient accessing services. Without a doubt, billing insurance can be a stressful at times, yet if a clear system is in place to manage the process it will ultimately result in more patients coming more frequently for care. The trick the practitioner must learn is how to dwell in this strange new world without compromising one's sanity.

Developing and maintaining proper perspective is essential to participating in the insurance dynamic in such a way as to have it enhance your quality of life rather than depleting from it. There is a big difference between the two! The biggest factor influencing your experience with insurance billing is how well you adjust your thinking and expectations and also moderate your emotional reactions when things don't cooperate.

It is inevitable with any system as complex as the insurance industry that frustrating challenges are going to come up again and again. To expect the insurance plans to ask "how high?" when you want them to jump is just plain unrealistic and you'll end up giving yourself a mental hernia trying to move something that big that isn't going to budge.

However, to quote a wonderfully eccentric colleague of mine, Christopher Huson, who is a professionally trained clown (as well as licensed acupuncturist): "The suits are miserable and they want us to be miserable too because misery loves company. But we are alternative medicine practitioners and we get to wear Hawaiian shirts to work".

When things get stressful we should be grateful that we get to help people and make a living doing it. The trick is not to leave a bunch of wreckage behind us in the process. One key to this is to have realistic expectations and a clear and efficient system for managing our end of this odd relationship with the insurance payers. The other key is to let go of what is beyond our control.

Hopefully this book will help you through the learning curve quickly so that you can find balance in your practice and take care of business so that business will take care of you.

Choosing a business model

When considering your business model there are basically three options to choose from: cash; superbill; or claims. There are great distinctions between these three very different ways of transacting business. There are also several key factors to evaluate in your decision-making process. Your decision should be based not just on the convenience factor (for you as well as the patient) but also on what your future goals are and how you can best reach them.

Everyone has a unique business plan and there is no right or wrong choice but it is important to pick the best path to further the success of your business. If you want to have a part time practice run out of your home and if you live in an area where patients can afford to pay what you charge then building a cash-based practice makes sense.

Additionally, if you are specialized in a certain technique or condition for which there is no common insurance coverage then there is no need to administer insurance billing. Examples of this would be facial rejuvenation acupuncture, fertility treatments, relaxation massage, wellness care, etc.

If your plan is to build a busier practice and you live in an area where patients want to use their insurance for reimbursement then you may want to consider helping them with this as it will make your practice accessible to a wider patient base. There are two options in this regard. The first one is similar to the cash-only practice in that your patients will still pay you at the time of service but you will now provide them with a form called a superbill that can be submitted by the patient to their insurance company for reimbursement for the payment they made directly to you.

Providing patients with a superbill will require you to code the services provided according to industry standard coding as well as adherence to a level of documentation in the medical record that will support the codes listed on the superbill. You also may be required to send copies of chart notes to the patient or their insurance plan to prove that the services for which the patient is seeking reimbursement were actually provided. Additionally, you may be asked to write a report or letter supporting the medical necessity of the treatment from time to time.

While there is more work required on your behalf, the main benefits of providing a patient with a superbill are three fold: The patient can be reimbursed for all or part of the cost of your services; your services are more accessible to a wider range of patients for whom insurance reimbursement is an important part of their decision to come see you; your cash flow is preserved by having your patients pay you "cash on the barrel head" for your services.

The third option is to dive in and file claims on your patient's behalf- they pay only their co-pay at the time of service or in many cases nothing at all. You file the claims directly to their insurance plan and then you wait for payment directly from the insurance payer.

While this option requires significantly more work from you it may be the right option if the following factors are important to you: you want to build a busy practice quickly and work more of a full-time schedule; many patients in your area have insurance coverage for your services and their plans provide higher benefit levels for "in-network" providers (more on this in the next chapter); there are other practitioners in your area that file claims for their patients and you want to be competitive by offering this service to your patients too; there are other practitioners in your area but no one else is billing insurance and you can create a unique advantage for patients to come see you instead.

Filing claims on your patient's behalf requires the most work on your part and also shifts your cash flow dependency to the random timing of insurance payments that often do not coordinate well with real-life expense needs. To mediate this you will need to create and maintain a clear system for filing and tracking claims, follow up on late claims and troubleshoot problems, spend time entering data into computer software, making more copies of chart notes, managing referrals and authorizations, and billing patients after the fact for unpaid balances due.

While the extra effort required to file claims on your patients' behalf may sound daunting, it can be managed efficiently and fit in to your weekly schedule in such a way as to not rob your soul or compromise your sanity. It requires having a clear system in place to manage the claims and track payments.

The main thing to remember is that by entering into a relationship with the insurance payers you are accepting that you will have to comply with their payment policies and be tolerant of their frequent tests of your patience. Making peace with this notion is at the root of staying in balance and not going crazy when things seem complicated.

Perhaps having a cash-only practice sounds pretty good to you. There are many practitioners who have taken the time to successfully nurture a cash practice to fruition. Maybe the middle-path option seems doable and your patients can afford to wait for reimbursement. However, if filing claims for your patients is the best model for your business then you owe it to yourself to set up a system that will work for you and your patients and this book will help you do just that.

Brave pioneers in states such as California and Washington have blazed a path into the world of in-network, contracted billing relationships with the insurance payers, with mostly mixed reviews. When a new state mandates insurance coverage for CAM services there is usually a rush by the larger insurance companies in that state to sign up as many providers as they can who agree to accept a discounted rate and strict utilization reviews. If you are in a state where no precedent has been set then it is imperative to proceed cautiously when the floodgates open.

It can be exciting to hear of the huge increases in patient volume that the insurance companies will supposedly be sending your way, however, it may serve you well to do some research and contact the state associations and individual practitioners in other states to assess their experiences prior to committing yourself to a potential spider's web that may be difficult to extricate from later.

Perhaps the ideal balance is found in the model where the patient pays the practitioner in full at the time of service and is given a receipt that can then be submitted by the patient to their insurance company for later reimbursement.

In areas where patients can't typically afford your services, however, and insurance coverage for CAM is prevalent, you may wish to submit claims for your patients. Remember that it is not required of you to be an in-network, contracted provider in order to submit claims for patients that have out of network benefits on their plan. Refer to the next chapter of this book for a more detailed explanation of the differences between "in" and "out" of network.

Out-of-network providers are not bound by contract terms that restrain the reimbursement rates and therefore are reimbursed based on their entire billed amount, whereas in-network providers are paid based upon the negotiated and discounted rates.

If there is no precedent in your area to join a network then why go there at all? This is the question that many practitioners in states where this is common are asking themselves. Not understanding what was at stake, many practitioners have signed low-ball contracts and unwittingly created a false economy for their valuable services that will continue to haunt all those that follow where they blindly stumbled.

18

"In" vs. "out" of network

If you have decided to play the insurance game then you will also need to decide whether to sign contracts to become an "in-network" provider or whether you will work as an "out-of-network" provider. Most insurance plans try to sign contracts with practitioners who agree to provide services to the insurance plan's members at a discounted rate.

The plans then provide financial incentives for the patients to utilize this network of contracted providers in the form of higher benefit levels. Conversely, patients will usually have to pay more money out-of-pocket if they see an out-of-network provider but the benefit to the out-of-network provider is that they are not limited in what they can be paid.

Health maintenance organizations (HMO's) and managed care plans generally restrict patients to only seeing contracted providers and many do not provide any benefits for services provided by out-of-network practitioners. If a majority of the patients in your area are covered by an HMO and you are willing to bill insurance then you should probably consider becoming a contracted provider.

This means accepting a discounted rate for your services, for which the plan will generally pay anywhere from

70-100% of the "allowed" (discounted) amount with the patient paying the difference between what the insurance paid and the agreed-upon, discounted rate. Often the patient's portion is a flat "co-pay" of anywhere from $5-30. Co-pays are subtracted from the total discounted rate and are not paid in addition to the discounted rate. This is important to remember. For example, if you normally charge $75, the discounted rate is $50 and the patient has a $25 co-pay, the insurance plan will pay $25. The difference between the discounted rate and your usual charge is written off by the provider and cannot be charged to the patient. This "write-off" is not tax deductible but a CPA can answer your questions about this more specifically.

Preferred provider organizations (PPO's) and plans that do not maintain a panel of contracted providers will permit their patient members to receive services out-of-network and will pay a certain percentage of the expenses. This means that it is not necessary to sign a contract in order to bill for treatments given to the plan's members. In general the member will receive a lesser reimbursement amount for seeing an out-of-network provider compared to one who is contracted and in-network. This typically ranges from 50-100%, with 50-70% reimbursement being most common. The difference between what the insurance plan pays and what the total charge is can be billed to the patient when the provider has not signed a contract agreeing to accept discounted rates.

Personal injury protection (PIP) is medical insurance for injuries resulting from an automobile accident. This is paid by the patient's own auto insurance company to the provider.

Unless the provider signs a contract with the insurance company or the company is listed as a participant in another network in which the provider is contracted then 100% percent of the usual charges may be expected to be paid. If PIP plans pay less than the full, billed amount, the difference may be billed to the patient unless prohibited by a contract. If the provider is participating in a discount network that represents multiple plans and by association the PIP plan is also a party to the contract, then the discounted rates prevail.

Worker's compensation, or labor and industries (L&I) coverage is insurance provided by the state or private plans for injuries resulting from a work-related incident. Generally a provider must be contracted with the state plan directly in order to submit claims although this can vary state to state. There is usually a discounted fee schedule and sometimes a unique set of billing codes that must be adhered to.

Rules for billing this type of insurance vary widely from state-to-state and it is suggested you contact your own state's L&I/worker's compensation benefits office to request the most up-to-date information.

Medicaid is a state run program for low-income patients. Most Medicaid programs currently do not offer CAM benefits but for those that do the rules are similar to the description in the paragraph above related to L&I.

Medicare is a federally run program for low income and/or elderly patients. Medicare currently has very limited CAM benefits and will not cover most CAM services until new legislation is passed by congress requiring coverage to be expanded.

You must contact Medicare directly to inquire about coverage for your services. If you qualify, then you must contract directly with Medicare and operate under extensive rules that can be quite restrictive and time consuming.

Obviously it would be ideal to charge your usual rate, be paid at the time of service, and hand the patient a superbill (more on this later) for them to send in to their insurance company for reimbursement. For patients who can afford this option- go for it! However, many patients cannot afford to pay as they go for an extended series of treatments and it is a great convenience to them if the provider will submit the claims and be reimbursed directly from the insurance plan, billing the patient later for any balance due. You can do this with any insurance plan that does not restrict the patient to only receiving services from a contracted provider.

If you decide to become a contracted provider with one or more plans or networks (networks represent multiple plans as a middleman) then you not only agree to accept discounted rates but you also must file claims directly as most contracts prohibit you from passing that responsibility to the patient.

A word about networks: there are many companies today who assemble a panel of providers who agree to discounted rates and utilization rules and then in turn contract with anywhere from one to over one hundred insurance plans (or even other networks) who then expect you to treat their patients and play by their rules. This can become quite complex in some cases when a PIP auto company or other insurance plan tells you that you must accept their discounted payment because they are contracted with a network you haven't even heard of which in turn is contracted with the network you actually signed the contract with.

The main thing to remember when considering contracting with any payer, plan or network is to look over the contract in detail and know what you are committing yourself to. Hiring a lawyer who is familiar with the language of these contracts can be invaluable. Your state professional association may also hire healthcare lawyers to evaluate new contracts and make recommendations on behalf of their members.

Just keep in mind that what you agree to may have repercussions not only for yourself but also for your profession as a whole. It is important to never accept what would amount to taking a step backward after all of the hard work that has gone into getting insurance plans to cover CAM services.

The first step in becoming a "preferred provider" is to contact the plan or network and speak with their provider relations or credentialing department. They will advise you as to whether or not they are accepting new providers at that time. If so, they will send you a credentialing application to fill out and return. Usually if you qualify they will activate you within 60-180 days.

If they are not accepting new providers at that time you may ask to be put on a waiting list, then when the panel opens again they will send you an application. In some cases you may be told that the panel is closed and the waiting list is also closed. You then will need to keep checking back with them once a month to try and catch them when the panel opens next. Most plans limit the number of providers proportionate to the number of members (patients) in a specific geographic region, county or state. While this can be frustrating, it is legal. If there are other practitioners in your profession who are still accepting new patients then it is hard for the plan or network to justify the expense of credentialing new providers. Once there is a need for more providers they will add more.

As unfair as it seems to new practitioners, it supports the basic idea of locating your practice in an underserved area where there is more need, and also protects existing practices from having to share a limited number of members with too many providers. In some cases you can get on a closed panel by joining an existing practice and working under their tax identification number. The rules for this vary by plan and can be found by contacting the provider relations department of the plan or network.

Remember, even if you can't get onto a panel of preferred providers, you may still bill as an out-of-network provider, assuming the plan provides out-of-network benefits. If this is the case, it may actually be an advantage as you will not need to accept the discounted rates the contracted providers must accept as payment in full- you can bill the difference to the patient.

Assessing the value of your services

Do you know what your time is worth? Knowing what to charge for your services is crucial to the success of your business. One very fundamental concept when deciding what your usual and customary charges will be is to always know what your cost per patient visit is. You are a business owner. You must run your business responsibly in order to stay in business. Never allow your rates to be lower than your cost per patient.

This chapter will walk you through an exercise that will help to calculate your average monthly expenses. You will then divide that number by your average number of patient visits in a given month to arrive at your cost per patient. This is your break even number. You won't make a profit unless you charge more than this number. You will lose money if you accept less.

One important reason to be aware of this number is that when you are considering signing a contract with an insurance plan you can compare your cost per patient with what they are offering to pay you. If, for example, your cost per patient is $75 and the plan wants to pay you $30 then you might as well hand each patient $45 as they walk through your door. You won't stay in business for long that way!

If you are a new practitioner and don't know how many patient visits to project for the purposes of this exercise just survey several practitioners you know that have been in business for 3 years or more and average their numbers. Statistics may also be available on your professional association's website. If this information is not available then use these numbers as a guideline: massage therapists may average 20 per week, acupuncturists 30 and naturopaths 50.

When estimating your own salary remember you will need to add up your personal monthly expenses and tax responsibilities. Include such things as your student loans, mortgage or rent, IRA & savings, child's tuition, insurances, food, tax deposits, in other words everything you spend in a month personally.

This exercise has nothing to do with what is tax deductible and what isn't. The sole purpose is to identify your total monthly expenses, both business and personal. For annual expenses such as malpractice insurance, accountant fees or business licenses, just divide them by 12.

What we'll do first is to add together all of your monthly expenses that are considered "fixed"- in other words, they don't vary month-to-month and are predictable. Then we'll add together the "variable" expenses for an average month, and finally, total your expenses. Add more items if they aren't already listed.

Fixed Expense	$ Amount	Variable Expense	$ Amount
Your salary		Medical supplies	
Office rent		Table paper	
Office staff		Dispensary	
Billing service		Laundry	
Business insurances		Office supplies	
Office utilities		Meals	
Equipment leases		Postage	
Telephone		Printing	
Cell phone		Credit card interest	
Internet		Continuing Ed	
Website hosting		Legal fees	
Bottled water		Accountant	
Subscriptions		Astrologer	
Advertising		Donations	
Professional dues			
Bookkeeper			
Janitorial			
Linen service			
Total Fixed Expense		Total Variable Expense	

- Add the totals for both categories and you'll have your total monthly expense.

  1 _____   Example: $8,000

- Write in your total number of patient visits for an average month.

  2_____   Example: 120

- Divide the number on line number 2 into the number on line number 1.

  3_____   Example: 67

- Total on line number 3 is the cost per patient visit.

In the example, based upon a monthly expense total of $8,000 and a monthly total of 120 patient visits then the cost per patient visit is $67. This amount will vary widely depending on your own individual circumstances and cannot be compared fairly to someone else's number. This represents the minimum average amount you must collect for a patient visit.

Now that you know what your cost per patient visit is you can go about the business of setting your fees so that your needs will be met. If you have a cash-only practice, you can break even charging a flat $67 per patient visit but your business will not show a profit or gain any equity, so if that is important to you (perhaps you'll want to sell your practice in 5 years) you may want to set your rate at $70, giving you a $3 profit margin per patient visit.

It is important to keep in mind that although one payer may offer less than your cost per patient visit, the difference may be offset by another payer who drives equal or greater patient numbers to you and who will pay more than your cost per patient visit, thus averaging out the reimbursement rate.

Stay aware of your payer mix to assure you are meeting your bottom line. Always keep your cost per patient visit in mind when evaluating a contract involving discounted rates for your services. Furthermore, because many insurance plans discount your billed rates when determining their reimbursement rates you will need to account for this difference and set your rates high enough to allow for the discount. One rule of thumb is to always adjust your fee schedule so that your billed charges are higher than what your highest payer is willing to pay.

Creating a fee schedule

If you run a cash practice then you can just set one fee for all of your patient visits, or for a few levels of service. However, if you bill insurance and provide multiple services or levels of service then you must determine how to value each service so that a typical patient visit will generate your target gross charge.

The way to do this is to organize all of your services and levels of service into a "fee schedule" that has associated charges for each item listed. A fee schedule establishes your "usual & customary" charges. These charges are what you bill to all payers regardless of what they actually end up paying.

It is legally required of practitioners to only maintain one fee schedule and not change their fees from payer to payer. Even though you may be contracted with 5 insurance companies that each pay you a different rate you must charge them all consistent with your usual & customary charges as listed on your fee schedule.

The first step is to compile a list of all services you can legally bill for according to your state's licensing law for your practitioner type. Contact your state licensing department for a current copy of your licensing law or contact you state professional association for assistance with assessing your scope of practice.

The current standard for organizing services for billing purposes is by using CPT codes. CPT stands for "current procedural terminology" and these codes describe specific services. CPT codes are published each year by the American Medical Association.

CPT codes are designed for the allopathic/Western biomedical community and are very limited when used to describe many CAM services. In the future there may be a new code set called ABC that will be CAM-specific, but for now CPT codes are the gold standard for billing insurance and all payers require their use.

Let's reference CPT codes in the context of how to value them when creating your fee schedule. It is important to have a clear rationale for setting your fees. Because of antitrust laws it is illegal for practitioners to agree to set rates with each other so you must generate your fees individually. You can pick your numbers because you like them and your numerologist blessed them, or by referencing federally assigned values from the Medicare system. Whichever method you choose just be sure it is a consistent system that generates fair values for your services.

Many practitioners reference the federal Medicare system's "relative value units" for each CPT code and base their fee schedules on this model. This is a good way to stay current with national economic trends and also be aware of geographic differences. The folks who create RVU's have done a huge amount of work to generate a numeric value for every CPT code. They take into consideration many factors ranging from the work expense of providing the service to the risk associated with a procedure and malpractice expenses.

The web address for downloading data files from the Centers for Medicare & Medicaid Services (CMS) at the time of this book's printing is:

http://cms.hhs.gov/providers/pufdownload/ and you will want to locate the most recent RVU file for physicians under the heading of "payment rates for non-institutional providers". It is titled "national physician fee schedule relative value file" and usually looks something like this: "RVU04_D.ZIP ". It will download as a zipped file and you will need Excel to view the spreadsheet format.

Once the zipped file is open the spreadsheet file will be titled something like "pprrvu04" and have a small letter "a" on the icon. Once the spreadsheet is open look toward column "L" or a nearby column with the heading "fully implemented non-facility". Then scroll down to codes in the 9xxxx series to find the most appropriate CPT codes that describe your services.

Once you have located the RVU for the CPT code you want to set a fee for you will need to multiply the RVU by what is called a "conversion factor". You can use the CF that is in the RVU file- which is the national Medicare standard, or you can make up your own CF in order to get the final number to be in a range that will meet your needs and achieve your target gross charge per patient visit.

As an example let's use a very common CPT code for massage therapy- 97124. In October 2003 the RVU for CPT code 97124 was 0.6 and if we multiply this number by the conversion factor of 36.7856 we get $23.27 for 1 unit (15 minutes) of massage therapy.

Another example uses the CPT code for the complex level of evaluation and management of a new patient, 99204. If the RVU for 99204 is 3.59 then when we multiply that number by the CF of 36.7856 we get $132 for this service.

Two exceptions to this are the CPT codes for manual and electro acupuncture: 97780 & 97781. The CPT code committee has never assigned RVU's to these two codes so if you are an acupuncturist you will need to make up your own RVU's that will give you the fee you want to charge when multiplied by the conversion factor you are using for other codes on your fee schedule.

While it is illegal to agree to set rates with other practitioners, it is fine to survey several practicing in your area to see what the range is in your geographic area for similar services. Then when you are deciding on the value for your CF you can price your fees accordingly. Some practitioners never go to the trouble of researching RVU's and they do just fine. Just pick a system that works for you.

A fee schedule is something that you should be able to hand to patients upon request, or present to an insurance payer you are credentialing with. Remember, you only have one fee schedule and so every payer you are billing is treated equally and fairly. Your fee schedule can be changed whenever you see the need and should be changed if your expenses increase or the next year's RVU's change, or your business plan changes. Fine-tuning your fee schedule at regular intervals is fiscally responsible and you can do this at any time.

A fee schedule for a massage therapist may only have two or three codes on it whereas a naturopath's fee schedule might have 60 or more and an acupuncturist would fall somewhere in the middle. The codes on your fee schedule depend upon your licensing laws, scope of practice and practice style. Not everyone will use the same codes. Everyone should, however, have fees that are consistent between the codes on their own fee schedule and that are based upon a defensible rationale that can be explained clearly to someone else.

An example fee schedule might look like this:

99203	New patient E/M	$100
99212	Established patient E/M	$50
97780	Manual Acupuncture	$100
97140	Manual Therapy (15 min.)	$30
97124	Massage Therapy (15 min.)	$25
97026	Infrared Therapy	$15

Again, a fee schedule is simply a listing of the services you normally provide along with the corresponding billing codes and your current fee for each service. If a prospective payer asks, you should be able to provide your rationale for your fees, such as the conversion factor you used or the usual and customary fee range for your geographic area.

Discounting

When practitioners are creating a fee schedule of billed rates they usually factor in the added expense of data entry, submitting a claim, managing accounts receivable, phone calls to follow up on late claims, time spent writing reports or photocopying chart notes, time spent reconciling payments and generating statements to patients or filing claims to secondary insurance, and then collecting these payments- usually in 45-90 days but sometimes 6 months or more.

Not having to manage a collections process can reduce your expenses dramatically. When a patient pays in full at the time of service you benefit from the immediate cash flow and the saved time and resources. Often the difference in actual cost savings for that patient visit is 10-20% or more. Unless you are a Medicare provider and bound by the federal Stark Act, which prohibits discounting, it is perfectly legal for you to extend a discount for "prompt payment", or a "time of service" discount.

Any discount is based upon your fee schedule of usual and customary charges, which is your one and only fee schedule. It is fine, however, to consistently apply a percentage-based discount, which reflects your cost savings by not having to bill, to all fees on your fee schedule. This is not a separate fee schedule- the amounts are discounted from your usual and customary charges.

Discounts can also be extended to any class of patients. Such as students, seniors, etc, but must extend to all patients within that class regardless of whether or not they have insurance coverage. In other words, if you give a student discount to your cash-paying patients, then you also have to bill the discounted rate to any other payer for that patient. The same idea is true of any promotional discounts you may be offering, such as 50% off a new patient visit- the patient with insurance is also billed at the discounted rate for that visit.

Similarly, this concept applies to the prompt payment discount. Some practitioners will extend the discount to anyone who pays within one week (or some other period of time) from the date of service. Some insurance companies may wish to make an arrangement with you to do this also, provided they also are charged the discounted rate for prompt payment.

The basic idea to keep in mind is that all payers are treated equally. If you bill your usual and customary charges to insurance plans then you also must bill the same charges for patients who are being billed and pay you after the prompt payment window of time has passed.

This fundamental concept of having one fee schedule that discounts are based upon, and relative to, makes it difficult for practitioners to have a flat rate for cash patients while billing multiple codes for insurance-covered patients that result in variable charges. As long as the insurance system continues to divide medical services into little "pieces of a pie" which then need to add up to the target gross fee, then we must continue billing with multiple codes. While this goes against the grain of holistic medicine it is the way it is.

What some practitioners do to simplify their discounted rates is to calculate their average gross billed charge and then calculate a discount amount relative to that value. This can apply to more extensive, first office visits and simpler return visits and you can generate two simple discount amounts that are relative to the gross billed averages. This makes it easier for your patients who choose to pay at the time of service so that they may plan ahead, knowing what the fee will be for each treatment.

One legal way for Medicare providers to do this is to join a discount program such as Simplcare, which provides the legal framework for you to maintain a separate fee schedule for cash patient who also participate in the program. More can be found about this program in the resources section at the end of the book.

Non-Medicare providers are not bound by the same federal rules regarding discounting and have more leeway. Check in with your state's attorney general and your sate professional association to find out if there are any local rules that may apply to discounting. The main thing to remember is that your system must have a defensible rationale and be easy to communicate.

Sliding scale fees are another option for practitioners who treat patients with varying abilities to pay for treatment. Again, it is important to have a defensible rationale for any sliding scale scheme and that it is applied consistently between patients.

Sliding scale discounts must be based upon an individual's income. They must earn less than a specified threshold to qualify, and the amount of the discount is relative to the amount earned. Documentation must be provided in the form of pay stubs or a recent tax return and an agreement should be signed. Their information should be re-verified every 6 months.

Some practitioners base their sliding scale thresholds on the federal poverty guidelines, which are published by the government annually. These can be found in a simple web search at the Department of Health and Human Services (DHHS) website. You can also modify the income criteria to better reflect the economic strata of your own community as long as it is fair and reasonable and applied consistently.

Some practitioners will also have their sliding scale patients list their average monthly debt payments as well as income and use a ratio between the two amounts to determine eligibility.

Discounts for prepayment of services has been found to be illegal in some states. In these cases practitioners offered patients a discount if they prepaid for a number of treatments to be used as needed. This was found to violate insurance laws in that it appeared the practitioner was operating similar to an insurance company without being licensed as an insurance company

However, if there is a set number of treatments indicated for a fixed period of time in order to execute a treatment protocol for an already diagnosed condition then that may be viewed differently. I t is encouraged that you consult a lawyer so as to not expose yourself to undue liability if you are considering offering pre-payment discounts.

Gift certificates generally do not qualify for a discount. They also cannot usually have an expiration date but that varies by state law.

An example discounting rationale is:

Average billed charges for new patient: visit:	$150
Less 20% discount for prompt payment:	$30
Total discounted charge for prompt payment:	$120

Average billed charges for return patient visit:	$100
Less 20% discount for prompt payment:	$20
Total discounted charge for prompt payment:	$80

An example sliding scale rationale is:

Patient income more than $xx.xx =	100% of rate
Patient income less than $xx.xx =	75-100%
Patient income less than $xx.xx =	50-100%

In addition to the above discounting rationales, some practitioners choose to give their patients a free treatment or two after a specified number of paid visits. There is nothing wrong with or illegal about giving away your services pro bono at any time. Just remember that all payers should be treated equally.

Maintaining financial health

It is important to evaluate your business at regular intervals. Giving your practice a financial check-up at six month intervals will help you make adjustments, when necessary, before things get too out of balance. It will also help you to stay on track with your business plan, see where you are straying from your plan, or when you might need to revise your plan to accommodate market forces that are beyond your control.

One aspect to look at is your payer mix. How many patient visits are attributed to each insurance payer? Is there one trouble plan that only sends you a few patients now and then yet requires an inordinate amount of your time? Perhaps you would be better of dropping that contract to free up your resources for other plans that are easier to deal with.

What does the balance between higher-paying plans and lower-paying plans look like? Are they averaging out to meet or exceed your cost per patient visit? If not, what can you do to tip the scales in your favor?

Another aspect to look at is what is called "charge capture". Are you billing for all of the reimbursable services you provide? If you regularly perform a service, even a small one, but aren't coding it and submitting it on the claim form with the other services then you are losing out on income that should be yours. Compound this omission over 12 months and a $10 service can add up to a significant amount after 1,000 patient visits.

One reason many practitioners don't capture all charges accurately is because they forget to document the encounter completely and then wait too long before charting and forget many details. Or perhaps they aren't aware of possible changes in their state law, or scope of practice law, that now permit them to bill for services that were not previously reimbursable.

On the other hand, changes can work both ways and it is important to not be billing for services that are not reimbursable or not within a provider's scope of practice.

Another area many practitioners get lazy in is their collections. It is easier to send out new claims than it is to stay on top of old ones that are aging. Assessing the state of your accounts receivables and doing regular audits will help you collect many balances due that otherwise will slip away. The longer you wait to collect the less your chances of actually getting an old claim paid. It is suggested that you check on the status of your aging claims every two weeks.

And finally, the area many providers overlook is controlling overhead costs. Sure, the new cell phone plan has internet access too, but is it really worth the extra $40 per month? Do you really need that new four color textbook set? How many bottles of the same vitamin formula do you really need sitting on your shelf? Did that full color, 6-page newsletter mailing bring you more patient visits than the free one you sent out via email? Is the yellow pages ad worth the extra $300 per month?

You can control your cost per patient visit in large part by keeping your expenses down. You have little control over how many patients actually come to you but you do have control over how much money your business spends.

In addition to controlling expenses, the other thing you can control is your productivity. Does your system require you to be fiddling around with things in the back office when you could be face to face with a patient? You can't bill for time you are not in the room with the patient so streamline your office system flow to maximize your billable hours. The more patients you see, the more money you make.

Common sense says to keep your income and expenses in balance with each other. Stopping to assess this at least twice a year will give you the clarity and big-picture perspective you need to run a sound business.

Coding for your services

Capturing all charges for the services you provide is essential to maintaining a healthy bottom line for your business. The way to do this is to understand how to code properly for the various components of a given date of service. Each reimbursable modality that you perform needs to be clearly listed on the claim form. If you perform services that are reimbursable without charging for them you are essentially giving money away.

In order to maintain a smooth flow of information through the various parts of the insurance system all services that are typically reimbursed by payers have been assigned a numeric or alphanumeric code. This standardizes the information to provide a consistent language that each party speaks.

Take the time to research all codes applicable to your modalities and list them somewhere for easy reference. Integrating them into your fee schedule or on a superbill-type of form is a good idea. Most billing software will also incorporate standard codes into pull-down menus for easy coding of claims.

As various states' scope of practice laws change and as billing codes are revised it is important to revise your own code set annually. Check with other practitioners in your area who are billing insurance and find out what codes they are using for the same services and compare these to existing CPT and ABC codes from the most current coding manuals available. Always keep in mind what services are within your legal scope of practice.

The best reference for CPT billing codes is the American Medical Association's "CPT" (standard edition) book, which is published each November for the following year. CPT stands for current procedural terminology. See the vendor list at the back of the book to locate a source for this and other resources.

Another source for billing codes is a code manual from Alternative Link that summarizes the new ABC code set, which is specific to CAM and nursing services. ABC codes are currently in a test phase and may become official after 2006. Until then the use of ABC codes as opposed to CPT codes depends on the payer you are billing and what codes they prefer you to submit. CPT codes are currently the national standard for billing codes and are accepted by all payers.

There are also a variety of "local" code sets used by different states workers compensation programs. Always reference a copy of the code set a payer wants you to use and code accordingly.

Worker's compensation code sets may utilize standard CPT codes, but often alter the codes for their own purposes or add additional codes for services not described in the standard CPT code set. One example is California workers compensation creating a specific code for cupping by an acupuncturist.

There are three types of CPT codes. One set is for procedures that are billed as one unit per day, for example, manual acupuncture-97780, is billed as 1 unit of acupuncture regardless of how long it takes to perform the acupuncture. Another example is a hot/cold pack-97010, billed at 1 unit.

The second type of CPT procedure code is time-dependant. These codes are billed in 15-minute units of time, with each 15-minute increment being represented by 1 unit. For example, massage therapy-97124, performed for 30 minutes is billed at 2 units, whereas 60 minutes is billed as 4 units.

The third type of CPT billing code does not describe specific procedures, rather, it describes evaluation and management (E&M) services such as performed by a naturopathic doctor or an acupuncturist to assess and diagnose a patient's condition and create a treatment plan.

E&M codes are very important to understand. It is crucial to use them properly and in the correct context. Generally massage therapists cannot bill E&M codes, and an acupuncturist's ability to use them varies widely from state to state depending on scope of practice laws.

In several states acupuncturists are considered diagnosticians and the language in their scope of practice law says so, thus they can bill E&M codes. However, in other states where acupuncturists must first obtain a referral from a physician prior to treating a patient, or be supervised by a physician, E&M codes cannot typically be billed.

Most states prohibit massage therapists from billing for E&M because their scope of practice is limited to performing procedures, not diagnosing. In this case the diagnosis code is usually provided by the referring physician. Ask other massage therapists in your area or your state association which codes they are billing or reference the CPT or ABC coding manuals for the latest codes.

Naturopaths have the widest scope of practice of the three CAM provider types and need to take the time to research all existing codes that describe their services. These can be found in the AMA's current CPT book or Alternative Link's ABC book. The clinic from one of the naturopathic colleges may also be able to provide you with their code set if they are in a state that has insurance coverage for ND's. Also, reference code sets from other local ND's to make sure you are not overlooking existing codes for reimbursable services you provide.

Acupuncturists are in perhaps the most unique position of the three provider types because there are many traditional modalities for which there are no CPT codes. While some CPT codes can be used to "get creative", this often creates problems and can trigger an audit.

The CPT code system was developed by physicians for physicians and as such offers little flexibility for non-western techniques. In general, if there isn't a CPT code for it, the service is non-reimbursable. The ABC codes offer much-needed relief in this regard but until they become standardized you are generally restricted to the existing CPT code set. If there is no existing CPT code for a service, you may petition the AMA's CPT code committee to create a new one, but until then the service is generally not considered reimbursable.

Which code set is accepted varies greatly from payer to payer. Always inquire as to the payer's preferred code type (CPT or ABC) before sending in a claim. Ask around to find out what codes other acupuncturists in your area are using successfully and which ones are causing problems. It can be a process of trial and error. What works with one payer may cause problems with another. For example, even within the same payer group, such as Blue Shield, some states claims offices consider 97781 (electroacupuncture) an investigational procedure and will deny claims for this service while others pay for it.

CPT codes for acupuncture services are found in the physical medicine section of the AMA's CPT manual and these codes, as such, are commonly considered the domain of physical therapists. Unfortunately these codes are also often reimbursed from the insurance plan's physical therapy benefit allotment, which is sometimes cause for friction between the two types of providers and a source of confusion for the patient but again, this is just the way it is.

Nobody ever said the system was perfect. These codes sometimes show up on a patient's explanation of benefits form (EOB) as "physical therapy" which can be confusing for the patient or their physical therapist but it is just the way the terms of that policy are structured. If your state's scope of practice law permits these types of services then these are the codes you should use. In this way, it can easily be explained to an ornery physical therapist who doesn't understand why you are billing "their" codes. There are also some cases where the CPT codes for acupuncture are listed as "surgery" for some reason on EOB's and patients may inquire about this. It's just another screwy part of the system and is no cause for alarm.

Naturopaths, by virtue of their training and much wider scope of practice, have many more codes at their disposal. Keep in mind that each state that licenses ND's has a different scope of practice that may restrict you from performing or billing for certain services. Do your homework and don't just assume that the codes referenced here are ok to use everywhere. Many CAM providers are audited by insurance payers and coding mistakes can prove costly. Know your state's scope of practice law and code accordingly.

For practitioners who are considered diagnosticians there are several groups of CPT codes used to bill for evaluation and management (E&M) services. Again, whether E&M codes are reimbursable for your license type depends upon your state's scope of practice law.

Generally, massage therapists cannot use these codes, while naturopaths should in almost every case and acupuncturists can in many states. Read your scope of practice law to see if it contains the word "diagnose". That will usually qualify you to utilize E&M codes.

How do E&M codes differ from the procedure codes discussed earlier? These codes describe time spent face-to-face with the patient taking a history, performing an examination, discussing a treatment plan, counseling the patient and managing their care.

An erroneous belief has been perpetuated among alternative practitioners that E&M codes are billed based on the amount of time spent with the patient. However, time is only one of several factors to consider when choosing the appropriate code level.

There are also many different categories of E&M code to choose from depending upon the location and context the service is provided in and whether the time is spent with the patient or in consultation with another medical practitioner discussing the patient's case. There are also different groups of E&M codes appropriate for CAM providers practicing in a non-hospital setting as well as a hospital or nursing facility setting.

It is the responsibility of the provider to code the patient encounter properly. It is up to you to be familiar with, and choose the most appropriate category and subcategory of service from the codes. The CPT code manual from the AMA offers an excellent tutorial on E/M coding.

If you plan on using these codes you should make the investment and learn how to use these codes responsibly. There are seven components used in defining the level of E/M service:

- History
- Examination
- Medical decision making
- Counseling
- Coordination of care
- Nature of the presenting problem
- Time

The first three of the above components (history, examination and medical decision making) are considered the key components when selecting the proper code level. An exception to this rule is when the visit consists primarily of counseling or coordination of care, in which case time is the determining factor.

Specific CPT codes are listed in the AMA's CPT manual and can also be found for free through an internet search or by asking your colleagues. The AMA wanted to charge $10 per copy of this book to include them here. In an effort to keep this book affordable for everyone they have been omitted.

Diagnosis coding is done using the International Classification of Diseases (ICD) system that is currently in its 9th edition. ICD9 codes are updated annually and it is important to be using the most accurate code for the diagnosis. These are used to describe conditions in Western biomedical terms, not alternative medical terms. There is no ICD9 code for "liver yang rising with kidney yin deficiency" while there is a code for "headache".

Unless your scope is quite broad and you are clearly able to diagnose internal medicine conditions using lab results and biomedical testing it is suggested you stick to ICD9 codes in the 7xx series. Codes in the 700's are generally descriptive of the locations of pain. An example is 724.2 for lumbar back pain. Many codes now go to 5 digits to specify specific joints or other details and it is essential to be as specific as possible.

Early in the year, you may find certain payers who have switched over to the latest ICD9 codes while other are still using the previous year's codes. If you get claims returned for incorrect diagnosis code call and ask which revision is being referenced.

Documentation & Charting

As you can see, quite a bit more goes into choosing the right E/M code than just the time spent with the patient during an encounter. As an exercise, read through the required components and then look through several of your patient charts. Pick out several dates of service and list all of the components present for those encounters. Select the most appropriate code for each one and then compare that to the code you actually billed. You might be very surprised at the result.

Besides only coding based on time, a common mistake many practitioners make is coding too low for a moderate case profile. Often, an encounter should be coded as a mid-level code but the practitioner guesses on the conservative side and down-codes. The other common mistake is to use too high a code level that is not supported by the documentation in the chart.

The key to utilizing E/M codes well is to have a good understanding of what components determine the code levels and to document the encounter accurately so that all of the necessary information is recorded which supports the level of code you chose. This is perhaps the least understood and most important point to remember when coding your services. If you perform services, but fail to document them, then you cannot bill for them. If it isn't in the chart then it didn't happen. Many practitioners get lazy or put off charting until a later time only to forget many details of the encounter. This just costs you money and wastes your time.

The other side of this coin is when there is a well-documented encounter, but too high of a code level is selected that is not supported by the information in the chart. Whether this is an act born out of ignorance, or a willful incident of upcoding, it constitutes billing fraud and is unethical and illegal. Trying to bill for services that are not reimbursable by using a higher-level code does not work either.

There are an increasing number of incidents where insurance plans are auditing charts for encounters their members had with alternative providers and they are finding numerous examples of inappropriate coding. These audits can result in high dollar-amount refunds for overpayments to the provider as well as termination of provider contacts and in some cases charges of insurance fraud.

Random audits may be inevitable, but the simple way to avoid getting into a bad situation as the result of an audit is to always document everything accurately and code based on the required components being present for the code level selected. Obviously you need to document any history taken, as well as examination findings and your diagnosis or differential diagnostic possibilities. You also should document the start and end times of the encounter, as well as what was discussed if counseling time is used to qualify a specific code level. The more complete the medical record is, the more confident you can be that, in the case of an audit, your codes will be solidly supported.

A great resource that goes into detail on the topic of charting and documentation is available in a book called "Hands Heal" by Diana Thompson. While primarily written for massage therapists, Diana's book is applicable for all CAM practitioner types and is a good companion to this Book.

Let's take a brief tour through charting basics. The standard format that everyone should be familiar with is the SOAP format: subjective; objective; assessment; and plan. Beginning with the patient's subjective description of the chief complaint and relevant history the practitioner then continues to document objective findings from the examination. Then the practitioner documents the diagnosis (or possible diagnoses if unclear) followed by the suggested treatment plan. If procedures are also performed during the same encounter they should be documented as well, including any start and end times for codes billed in 15-minute units.

It is also important and appropriate to document patient compliance with the treatment plan or if the patient is not complying with or finding the treatment to be effective. Having an objective, number-based scale for the patient to report how they feel at each encounter will provide you with a visible track record showing any improvement, or lack thereof, in the patient's presenting problem. This is very useful when justifying medical necessity for the continued treatment of a patient's chief complaint when an insurance plan performs a utilization review.

If any counseling occurs during an encounter and the counseling constitutes great than 50% of the total time spent face to face with the patient, this should also be documented with start and end times, as well as what was discussed. Only information relevant to the presenting problem should be documented. If you spend 10 minutes talking about the patient's recent vacation or the health of their pet, this obviously cannot be included in the time being billed and does not constitute counseling services. On the other hand, discussing risk factors and performing risk factor intervention through patient education should be well documented to support the E/M code selected.

Counseling in this context is not the same as psychotherapy and different CPT codes are used. For the purpose of insurance billing and specifically for the use of E/M codes regarding counseling, the following definition of counseling is the standard: counseling is a discussion with a patient and/or family concerning one or more of the following areas:

- Diagnostic results, impressions, and/or recommended diagnostic studies.
- Prognosis.
- Risks and benefits of management (treatment) options.
- Instructions for management (treatment) and/or follow-up.
- Importance of compliance with chosen management (treatment) options.
- Risk factor reduction.
- Patient and family education.

As you can see, having a good system in place in your office that supports timely, accurate and complete documentation is essential in order to be reimbursed for the services you provide. Having pre-formatted chart templates is a way of organizing the information-gathering process that many practitioners find helpful. Other practitioners use dictation software that converts their speech into a word processing document that an office staff member later references to code the encounter. Whatever system you choose, apply it consistently in a timely fashion and constantly seek ways to improve it to yield charts that are easy to read, and which contain all of the information necessary to support the codes you are submitting.

The "golden rule" of billing is quite simple: "Do what is <u>medically necessary</u>, completely <u>document</u> what you do and accurately <u>code</u> what you document".

Ethical issues in insurance billing

Ethical issues are cause for much discussion when billing insurance is concerned. It is easy to let emotions lead you into behaviors that may be counterproductive in the bigger picture. While dealing with the insurance industry can be frustrating at times, it is important to remember that each time you send in a claim and sign a contract you are volunteering to participate and are not a hapless victim. It is always your choice. Yes, it will often feel like an unfair relationship, rife with seemingly purposeful roadblocks, yet to allow resentment to lead you into ethically vague activities runs counter to the spirit of being an alternative medicine provider.

The insurance industry is such a huge institution that expecting it to change for a handful of CAM providers is very unrealistic. To participate in billing insurance on behalf of your patients means that you, not the insurance industry, will be making changes. Accepting that this just comes with the territory and is part of the new landscape in which we find ourselves makes it a little bit easier to function efficiently.

For many CAM providers it is no longer a black and white proposition: bill insurance or go completely cash. As an increasing number of patients have coverage we are finding that offering to bill their insurance for them is a valuable service that may allow them to access CAM services that they would not otherwise be able to afford. Obviously we are not billing insurance for our own benefit. It is an open-hearted service to our patients. Keeping this perspective is imperative to staying in balance and sane when problems inevitably occur.

One issue that frequently confounds CAM practitioners who treat the patient holistically is the concept of "medically necessary" care. In our view all care is medically necessary, especially preventive care and maintenance care. In the definition of the insurance industry, the phrase "medically necessary" refers to care for a specific, diagnosed symptom that is relatively acute in nature, which meets Western biomedical standards of care for the condition, and which responds to treatment in a timely fashion and reaches a point of resolution.

Continuing to bill for treatment of a condition that has reached a plateau no longer meets the definition of "medical necessity", nor does preventive care or "wellness care". Billing insurance for these services is unethical by the terms of the contracts you sign as a provider. To hide the real reason for treatment behind a diagnosis code for a secondary ache or pain is not only unethical, it can constitute insurance fraud.

To document "medical necessity" you should show: any available hard data such as imaging test results, lab results, etc; decreased use of medications; decreased use of other services; decreased time loss from work; decreased return visits; improved function- for example- can sit for 60 minutes, walk for 2 miles, go up stairs, etc.

Obviously, wellness care is a significant part of a healthy CAM practice and our patient's lives. It is important, however, to educate our patients from the first visit that "total wellness" is not a covered service according to the insurance industry. You must identify and differentiate the services you provide that are "wellness" from those that are "medically necessary" on your office policy forms. Set the stage to build the wellness aspect of your practice with good patient orientation and appropriate waivers for non-covered services.

Obtain written consent from the patient for non-covered services prior to providing services and/or supplies that fall outside of the definition of "medical necessity". If you obtain the consent you can bill the member for things such as: non-covered services; investigational services; non-participating lab charges; supplies. The member's consent must include, at a minimum: a description of the specific service; date of service; cost of service and why the service was not covered by the insurance payer; member name and signature; documentation must be available upon request.

Another issue that is a hot button for providers is the issue of reimbursement rates. By signing a contract as a "preferred provider" you are agreeing to accept a heavy discount from your usual and customary charges. Attempting to offset this by using a higher code level than is appropriate based upon services rendered (known as "up-coding") is unethical and can constitute insurance fraud. If you simply cannot live with the rate you are receiving without resorting to this unethical practice, then perhaps you should reevaluate your participation with that particular payer.

Other examples of inappropriate billing include: billing for services rendered by someone else; billing for services not rendered; intentional misrepresentation of the diagnosis, procedure code, date of service or level of care; concealing non-covered or limited services with E/M codes.

Keeping a somewhat detached perspective on the whole affair is crucial to not letting insurance billing distract you from your real purpose of helping your patients.

Audits

The word "audit" strikes fear into the hearts of many providers who do not understand how to code and document services correctly. For those who are prepared an audit can be a painless experience. An audit is when an insurance company reviews billing records, coding patterns and chart notes for patients who are members of the insurance company's plans. The plan can only review charts of their own members and cannot see records pertaining to other patients.

Typically they will look back over charts for the previous two years, although in some cases they may go back further. Your signed contract as a preferred provider most likely contains a section giving them the right to audit your records at any time as long as it does not interfere with your normal course of business.

Some practitioners are audited at random, however, most audits are triggered by certain billing patterns that raise a red flag for the claims processing department. Several issues that can trigger an audit are:

- Contracting issues
- Billing for non-covered services
- Utilizing unlicensed practitioners

- Billing for non-credentialed practitioners
- Office materials state that treatments provided in your office are for "wellness care"
- Handouts do not segregate covered vs. non-covered services
- Charting issues
- Unknown initials or practitioner
- Insufficient notes and/or documentation
- Documentation does not show treatment is related to diagnosis
- Reassessment and progress report not in chart and care appears maintenance
- Billing issues
- Incorrect ICD9 and/or CPT codes
- ICD9 doesn't link to CPT code
- High utilization of codes 99214 & 9915
- Billings do not reflect actual provider of service
- Services billed do not fit bell curve profiles for provider type

As far as billing for non-covered services, this can trigger audits when it happens regularly. Always verify with the payor that they consider your modalities to be medically necessary. Often a technique you wish to bill for is determined to be investigational and thus deemed non-reimburseable. These can include things such as feldenkrais, visceral manipulation, chelation therapies, toyo hari, even electroacupuncture in some cases.

Physical rehabilitation services should always have a treatment plan available that includes appropriate and legible chart note documentation; physician prescription or referral (if needed); documentation that supports the following- level of care provided, medical necessity of care provided, and that procedures performed are within scope of practice.

As far as specific codes, in general, codes ending in a "9" will result in a request for chart notes and/or a report and can trigger an audit as well as building your profile as an "outlier". An outlier is a practitioner who shows a billing pattern that deviates from the norm for other providers of the same type within the same community. Services and billing patterns are summarized to create bell curves by provider type. Practitioners who fall outside of the bell curve are considered outliers and will be audited.

It may be the case that the practitioner designated as an outlier is just undereducated about current billing & documentation standards, or it can indicate fraudulent behavior. Each year large health plans terminate the contracts of about 40 providers who fail audits and are deemed to be billing fraudulently. In some cases very large sums of money are retracted in the form of retroactive refunds for overpayments and penalties. In extreme cases legal penalties have been levied against individuals and the institutions they work for. It pays to get it right the first time!

A service some practitioners find helpful in verifying that they are submitting the best codes for their services is CodeCorrect. This is a web-based service that costs about $30 per month and offers a free trial to see if it will be of use to you. If you are billing many different codes and managing a high volume of complicated claims then this type of service could be very helpful in preventing your claims from triggering red flags and audits. There are also certified medical coders who can review your claims for you. Many larger clinics have a coder on staff in the insurance department.

Verifying Benefits

One of the most important things you need to do when you are billing insurance is to verify the benefits of the patient's plan before proceeding further. Many patients will tell you that they already know that their plan covers alternative medicine but it is absolutely necessary that you call and verify the benefits yourself. Never take the patient's word when it comes to insurance. They usually know even less than you do!

There are several questions you will need to get answers to so it is a good idea to create a checklist of these questions to guide you when you are on the telephone. A suggested checklist is included on the optional companion Cdrom and can be modified to suit your needs.

Start by calling the telephone number on the patient's insurance identification card. Usually it is labeled "benefits & verification" or "member services". Do not call the number for hospital pre-certification or prescription drug benefits. Many times you will find yourself in a virtual maze of voice mail options. When this happens it is best to call back and then don't press anything, waiting for a live human to come on the line. Then tell them you are a provider and you need to speak with a customer service representative. In some cases just pressing "0" will connect you to a live person.

Automated benefits systems that offer to fax you a summary of benefits will not do you any good. They don't include information about CAM benefits. It is always important to get through to a live person. Sometimes when this seems impossible it may be because the company you are calling is in a different time zone and it is outside of normal business hours but instead of telling you this they will unintentionally trap you in voice mail hell. Other times they may be closed for storms or holidays.

Be prepared for these calls to take some time, either while on hold waiting to get through the queue or on hold while the representative hunts down the CAM benefits for the member's plan. Once you do get through to a live person the first thing you need to do is to document the time & date of the call and the name of the representative. In the event of conflicting information later on in the billing process you can point to this documentation to defend your claims. Many times they will record the call or at least write notes in the patient's file for later reference. In some cases this is proof enough to overturn denied or unpaid claims. You will find that it is not uncommon for the rep to tell you one thing, only to have the adjuster who actually processes your claim deny it, so this is a very important step to not skip over.

If you have called the particular company before and are familiar with the general benefits of their plans, yet a representative sounds unsure and is giving you information that sounds strange, call again right away. You will almost always get through to a different person who may very well give you a different answer. If you are getting conflicting or confusing information ask to speak with a supervisor

It is important to be very clear with your questions and not let them rush you through the call before you get all the answers you need. Out of state plans are especially difficult to deal with as they frequently have different state laws governing CAM benefits and are not familiar with the local mandates of your state.

If your state law requires coverage, but they say there is none, it can be helpful to remind them of your state's laws. They will usually put you on hold while they research this and then change their tune when they see it in print. Ask them to note this in the patient's file so it can be referenced later if necessary.

Because benefit levels can vary significantly depending on whether a service is offered by an in-network or out-of- network provider it is good to verify your status with that plan. Sometimes a company will have multiple plans and you may be listed as in-network for some but not all. Ask them to find you in their system by using your tax ID number. Mistakes can happen and if you are contracted with a middleman network that "forgot" to forward your data to the plan, then they will not pay at the highest level of reimbursement. It is good to know up front if a problem exists so you can take care of it sooner rather than later when it always causes more problems.

Verify that the plan will cover the specific CPT codes you plan on billing. Even though one state might cover acupuncture, they may only cover the code for manual acupuncture and not the code for electro-acupuncture.

Finding this out right away will save you the time it takes to go through an additional billing cycle when you have to resubmit the claim. Another example is a massage therapist who might perform a variety of techniques and usually bills 97124, only to find that a particular plan will only cover 97140 and deny claims for the other code. Since these codes can be used interchangeably for many techniques it is good to know up-front which one will get paid and which one will cost you more time.

You should also ask if the plan covers your services for the condition being treated. You don't need to give a specific diagnosis code but it can help to be as specific as possible. Most insurance plans will not cover relaxation treatment or preventive care, but will cover pain-related services. They usually have a list of covered and non-covered diagnoses for CAM providers. They will always begin and end the call with the caveat that all claims are subject to approval based on medical necessity.

Always ask if a referral or authorization is needed. A patient may need to present to you a prescription from an MD or similarly licensed physician before the plan will cover your treatments. In this case you should submit a photocopy of the script with every claim.

Sometimes a doctor's office will insist that an Rx is all that is needed when in actuality they need to generate a referral through the insurance plan's system that is kept on file there. Inquire about this very specifically if you are told the patient needs a referral. If the plan requires authorization of the referral then the referring physician must submit the authorization request directly to the insurance plan, not to you. If it isn't on file at the plan then it doesn't exist and they won't pay it.

If an authorization is required the insurance plan will send a paper copy of the authorization to you after it has been approved and the data has been loaded into their system. This can take up to a week or more and it can be frustrating to wait to begin treatment if the patient needs attention quickly. It is important, however, to at least have the authorization number before providing the first treatment unless you have been instructed otherwise by the plan. You can call and get this number over the phone before the paper copy makes its way to you through the mail.

If a patient insists on beginning treatment right away then there is a risk that the services will not be authorized and subsequently not covered, leaving the patient with a bill and you in the position of being stuck in the middle. If you decide not to wait for the authorization before beginning treatment then you must tell the patient there is a good chance the plan will not cover it and in that case the patient will be responsible for all charges. As always, have the patient sign an agreement of financial responsibility. Never tell a patient that there won't be a problem or that the treatments will be covered just because you've billed their plan hundreds of times before. For some reason when you do that a cosmic law of irony kicks in and a problem inevitably occurs.

When they tell you a referral is needed, get a referral. If an authorization is required, get it authorized. It may take time, but it will save you from all sorts of potential hassles further on down the line. Do it right the first time. Most plans and many doctors will not generate an authorization or referral retroactively so be sure all the paperwork is in order before beginning treatment.

Another question for you to ask is if the plan has any licensing restrictions. For example, there are some plans that will only cover massage when done by a physical therapist, or acupuncture only when performed by an MD, or manual manipulation only when done by a DO or DC. It can be easy to forget this point when the fast-talking customer service representative tells you the patient's plan does indeed cover acupuncture, only later to find out they actually only cover it when performed by an MD. You'll wish you had known that before giving 10 treatments to the patient.

You will also need to know if you should collect a "co-pay" from the patient at the time of service. Some plans that you are contracted with will specify that the patient's portion is limited to a fixed dollar amount, commonly from $5 to $30. Other plans will provide coverage for a percentage of the reimbursement amount, usually 70-100% of allowed charges for an in-network provider and 0-100% for an out-of-network provider. You'll also want to know if there is any unmet deductible so that you can advise the patient of their potential out-of-pocket costs.

You will need to know what the maximum coverage is for your services. Generally this is limited on a calendar-year basis. Plans will often limit coverage to a max number of treatments per year or per condition. Coverage is also frequently limited by dollar amount- sometimes as little as $150 per year. Increasingly, plans are starting to lump together different types of CAM services so that $500 or so is allocated for all CAM treatments. In this case, if the patient has already seen a chiropractor 30 times before showing up on your doorstep, chances are good that the benefits have been exhausted. Inquire about how much is remaining in the pot and ask the patient about their treatment history for that year. Once a patient's benefits have been exhausted they are treated like a non-insurance patient unless restricted by the terms of a contract you may have with the plan.

Finally, and very importantly, ask where to send the claims! Often the address shown on the patient's card is out of date, or the company has CAM claims sent somewhere else first. Some companies have several different plans or large employer groups that each will require the claims to go to a specific address for processing. Always double check, even if you have sent a dozen other claims in for that company.

Patient financial responsibility

Let's define a few terms that are fundamental to understanding the patient's financial responsibility: co-pay, co-insurance and deductible. While some health plans will cover 100% of the fee, most plans require the patient to pay a portion of the total cost. This portion is referred to as their "co-pay" or a "co-insurance percentage". Some plans also require the patient to pay an initial, annual dollar amount out of pocket before the insurance begins paying anything- this is called a "deductible". We'll go through each of these concepts one-by-one so that you can fully understand how these work in reality.

It is common for insurance plans to require the patient to pay out of pocket for services up to a specified threshold before the insurance begins paying anything. This is the deductible. A deductible amount varies by plan and usually ranges from $200 on a standard plan to as high as $10,000 for a major medical plan. This amount resets at the beginning of each calendar year and until the reimbursable amount reaches this threshold the insurance will not pay anything. You should know what the patient's deductible amount is, having received this information when you verified their benefits.

Many patients are confused about what a deductible is, how much their deductible is, and are often surprised to find out that they have one at all. Some plans have one deductible for general medical care, with a separate deductible for CAM services. Know what the patient's deductible is and discuss this with them so they are not surprised when they receive a bill from you for the full reimbursable amount if their deductible has not been met for the year.

Sometimes, if you know exactly what the insurance company's fee schedule is for the codes you are billing, you can ask the patient to make a payment at the time of service. Usually, however, it is better to submit the claim and wait for the explanation of benefits form to arrive, which will indicate exactly how much the patient is responsible for. If there is concurrent care with other providers it is impossible to predict whose claims will be processed first and which claims will be applied to the deductible.

Once a patient's deductible has been satisfied for the calendar year they are usually only responsible for a co-pay or co-insurance percentage. If you are a contracted, in-network provider then there will probably be a specified dollar amount per service for which the patient is responsible. It is prudent to collect this amount at the time of service. Collecting even $5 or $10 can buy your lunch on that day and help your immediate cash flow. Co-pays are much harder to collect after the patient has left the office. Most contracts require you to collect this co-pay amount and it cannot be waived as per terms of the contract. Co-pays are increasingly growing each year to as much as $25 or $30 in many cases. This can represent a significant portion of the total reimbursement rate under some contracts. Be sure to collect it!

The co-pay amount is subtracted from the total reimbursement amount so that the amount paid by the insurer will be less than the rate specified on the contracted fee schedule by the same amount as the co-pay. For example, if the reimbursement rate is $60 and the co-pay is $25 then the patient pays you $25 and the insurance payer should pay you the $35 balance. Do not make the mistake of thinking the co-pay amount is in addition to the reimbursement rate specified in your contract.

Many plans, rather than having a set dollar amount, specify a percentage of the total reimbursement rate for which the patient is responsible. This can range from 10-50% in most cases. This is a co-insurance percentage. Out-of-network practitioners will be reimbursed based upon a percentage of the total charges submitted, while contracted providers percentages are based upon the negotiated, discounted amounts specified in the fee schedule for that contract. Again, contracted providers are generally bound to collect this amount due from the patient and it cannot be waived. Non-contracted practitioners, however, are not bound by contract in this regard.

Like co-pays and deductibles, co-insurance percentages that are the patient's responsibility are indicated on the explanation of benefits form you will receive from the insurance payer. If you know exactly how much the reimbursable amount is for a particular payer you may collect the patient's portion at the time of service, but because the final dollar amount is frequently unknown until after the fact, it is often better to wait and bill the patient later. That said, whenever possible, have the patient make a payment at the time of service in order to ease the pain of having to wait 30 or more days for the balance to be paid by the insurance payer.

For indigent patients or those experiencing financial hardship, the Department of Health and Human Services issued an advisory statement saying that it is ok for the provider to waive the deductible and co-pay amounts. First, however, be sure to verify whether or not this waiver is prohibited under the terms of your contract with the patient's health plan. Many contracts will not allow you to waive the patient's financial responsibility.

Information management

Managing the information needed to successfully process claims and ultimately receive payment is crucial to the success of your business. From the first step of photocopying the patient's insurance ID card to the final step of reconciling a payment you will need to manage many pieces of information and have it organized in such a way that you can easily find something in a hurry. More claims than I care to think about have required some extra work in order to be processed. Having a neat, simple and efficient system of storing and tracking this information will make your life much easier.

Schedule regular time to enter data, generate claims and reconcile payments. It really doesn't take very long to do this but if you let a large pile accumulate on your desk it will seem daunting to even get started, and the longer you procrastinate the bigger the pile grows. This aspect of your business can be intimidating at first. Hang in there, maintain a simple, clear system, and once you get used to it you will probably find that it really only requires a few hours per week.

My photocopier, fax machine, computer and filing cabinet have become indispensable pieces of equipment in my office. They are as important to the success of my business as my acupuncture needles and massage tables. Put some forethought into creating your information system rather than reacting to a flood of information requests while in crisis mode after the fact.

After I photocopy the patient's insurance ID card (front and back) and call to verify benefits I staple the card copies, benefits verification checklist and the patient's insurance intake form together. I then enter the patient's info (and the insurance company info if it is new to my system) into my billing software. The hard copies go into the back of the patient's chart, which is filed alphabetically in a locked file cabinet. I also file copies of referrals or authorizations in the same manner.

Every time I generate a new claim or statement, or a payment is made, I enter this into the computer. If I need to I can print out a clear statement of the patient's account at any time. I also have a file folder for the explanation of benefits forms that accompany payment checks, this way I can deposit the checks quickly for cash flow and reconcile the payment against the claim at a later time when I can process a batch of claims together. After the claims and payments have been reconciled I file the explanation of benefits (EOB's) forms chronologically in large folders in case I need to reference them later. If I am billing secondary insurance for a patient I will photocopy the EOB's from the primary payer and keep these in the back of the patient's chart until the secondary payment has been received.

I batch process multiple claims at one time and have pre-printed envelopes with address windows that match the claims forms address panel placement so that I can just print, fold, stuff and stamp in a matter of seconds. I also have smaller envelopes with my address printed on them that I include with patient statements to make it that much easier for them to return their payment promptly. These supplies are readily available and surprisingly affordable and will make your billing process so much easier than piecing it all together. A list of reliable suppliers is in the back of the book.

One last thought on the topic of information management- it goes unsaid a lot of the time because it is so basic and yet many people don't do it: back up your computer files every single time you update a record or make changes! Back them up on an external storage medium such as a CD-RW or a Zip disc. Never rely on backups made to your hard drive. Take your backup disc home with you each evening.

Protecting your information is crucial, not only for patient privacy and HIPAA compliance, but for the future of your business. Many times a payer will need more information from you or a claim will have to be resubmitted well after the original date of service. If you can't find the needed information then you are out of luck.

Claim forms and superbills

Claim forms and superbills are the nuts & bolts of insurance billing. Without a clearly formatted vehicle to deliver the necessary information to the payer the entire system would break down. When sending claims from a practitioner's office directly to an insurance payer it is frowned upon to make your own form as it slows down the time it takes to process your claim and increases the likelihood of the claim getting lost in the shuffle.

Over the years the Medicare system has refined a typical claim form into one standard format that is universally accepted by all payers. Formerly known as the "HCFA" form, it is now called the CMS 1500 claim form- the classic, red ink on white paper form that looks confusing at first but which is really quite simple once you become familiar with it.

Most payers are now automatically scanning CMS 1500 claim forms into software that electronically processes the claim. This is why having one standard format is so important. If you are going to be sending claims to insurance payers from your office you should use these forms. They can be purchased in bulk from most medical supplies distributors.

All claims software programs will print the claim data into the correct boxes on the blank CMS 1500 forms for you. Some software programs will also print the entire form onto a blank white sheet of paper, but the cost of the extra ink toner required to do this quickly outweighs the cost of purchasing bulk forms and feeding them through your printer as needed.

Again, if you are using a software program for your billing it will automatically fill in the required fields on the CMS 1500 form for you. If you must fill these forms in by hand consult the online tutorial at your payer's website for detailed instructions. Be very careful to keep the data aligned within the appropriate form fields as this is a common error.

One alternative to a CMS 1500 form when you just need to give the patient a receipt is a superbill. This is what you hand to a patient when they pay you directly and need something to send in to their insurance company to obtain reimbursement. A superbill can be as simple or complex as you want to make it but it needs to contain specific information in order for the claim to be processed efficiently.

A superbill should be easy to read and should contain the patient's name, date of birth and insurance identification number as well as the practitioner's name and address, license number and contact information. The ICD diagnosis code(s) and CPT or ABC services codes should be marked, as well as the charge for each associated code. The total amount paid by the patient should be indicated as well as the date of service. The practitioner should sign the form.

When using superbills, it is nice to give the patient two copies so that they can keep one for their records and send the other in to the insurance company. It is also a good idea to keep a paper or electronic copy on file in your office for future reference.

Your local printer can make pre-printed, carbonless, duplicate or triplicate superbills for you at a very reasonable cost. Superbills can also be ordered from many medical supply distributors and easily be customized with your billing codes, logo and contact information on them. Examples of a superbill (or charge slip) template can be found on the optional, companion CDrom and also at www.MedicalArtsPress.com or from many other forms suppliers.

Explanation of benefits

The explanation of benefits (EOB) form is what you receive from the insurance payer in response to the claim you submitted. It provides a summary of the submitted codes & charges, adjusted amounts, amounts the patient is responsible for paying and the amount the insurance payer has either paid you or applied toward the patient's deductible. The EOB provides crucial information for you to use when it comes time to reconcile the claims you have submitted with the payments made and balances remaining. Reading the EOB carefully can also show you when the insurance payer has made a mistake, such as incorrectly processing the claim or even having the wrong tax identification number on file for you.

Most EOB's are formatted similarly, with one or more dates of service on one or several pages. Some are printed on both sides of a page, so don't forget to turn each page over and take a look! An EOB may also combine information about claims for several different patients. If a check has been issued and is in the envelope with the EOB it will represent the sum of all of the claims on the EOB even if they are for multiple patients and/or dates of service. Make sure the amount of the check matches the total dollar amount indicated on the EOB. It can be helpful to note the check number when crediting payment toward each patient's account in the event that future questions about payment arise.

To read the EOB, begin by finding the patient's name and the date of service, usually found in a column on the left-hand side of the page. If you billed multiple codes for a single date of service they will each have a row beginning with the date of service, then the code or service description. Following the row from left to right you will see the billed charges next and then the adjusted amount, which is the difference between what you billed and the insurance payer's reimbursement rate. Next you will see the portion of the reimbursement rate for which the patient is responsible, such as a co-pay or co-insurance percentage. Finally, the amount paid by the insurance payer will be displayed, or whether this amount has been applied to the deductible. If any, or all, of the amount due has been applied to the deductible then the enclosed payment check will be short by this amount. You can see why reconciling with the EOB is essential to your bottom line when there are significant patient portions due.

If there is a secondary payer on file for your patient, then any remaining balance should be billed to this other payer so keep the EOB handy for future reference as a copy of it must be submitted with the new claim form in order to properly coordinate the benefits between the two payers.

Coordination of benefits

The term "coordination of benefits" refers to the process of billing two different insurance payers for the same patient. Some patients will be covered on a primary plan from their own employer and also have secondary benefits under their spouse's plan from a different employer. If the patient's own plan, referred to as the "primary" plan, has a co-pay or coinsurance percentage, then this amount is usually not paid for by the patient but by the spouse's plan, referred to as the "secondary" plan. In other cases the primary plan may be the patient's PIP automobile insurance, Medicare, or Worker's Compensation, with the patient's own health insurance taking the role of the secondary plan when the condition being treated is due to an auto or work accident or the patient is eligible for Medicare and has a supplemental private policy.

In order to efficiently coordinate benefits between two plans you must have the information not only for the patient but for their spouse as well, or in the case of an auto or work accident or Medicare, the necessary billing information and claim numbers for these plans. Photocopy both insurance cards and verify benefits with both plans, including where to send the claims. Obtain the correct spelling of the spouse's name along with their date of birth and member identification number complete with any alpha-prefix.

In the case where the patient and their spouse are both insured, you will first send the claim to the patient's own insurance plan as this is the primary payer. Once you have received the EOB from the primary payer, then you may submit a second claim that is identical to the first one (with the addition of any new payments made) to the spouse's plan, this being the secondary payer. In addition to showing the amounts paid on the claim form, you need to attach a copy of the primary payer's EOB with applicable lines of information highlighted. Be sure to black out any identifying information about other patients who might have also been included on the EOB in order to protect their privacy. In addition, on the top of the claim form you may hand write "secondary claim" and "attachment enclosed".

In the case of a PIP auto insurance or worker's compensation claim, these would be the primary payer, and the patient's own plan is the secondary payer. The spouse's plan, if any, would be third in line. Any unpaid balances remaining after the PIP auto company or worker's compensation have made payment should be sent to the patient's health insurance or paid by the patient directly at their option. Again, the same process for submitting the secondary claim applies here.

As far as Medicare is concerned, very few CAM services are actually covered benefits under the current Medicare system. If there are benefits for your services and you are obligated to bill Medicare, then Medicare is the primary payer. If the patient has a Medicare "supplement" plan then this is considered the secondary payer once Medicare has paid its maximum level of benefits. As in the first two examples, follow the same procedure for submitting the secondary claim.

If Medicare does not cover your services, such as is the case with acupuncture, then you will need to send the denial letter from Medicare, along with the claim form, to the secondary plan. It may be easier, as well as saving you a lot of time that would otherwise be spent waiting for the denial letter to show up, to just keep a denial letter from Medicare on file and send a copy of it directly to the secondary plan with claims and bypass sending the claim to Medicare altogether.

After you have reconciled EOB's from the various payers, any balance still remaining should be billed directly to the patient. This, of course, does not include any amounts adjusted under your provider contracts if this is prohibited under terms of the contract. If you are not require to write-off the adjusted amount, such as in the case of a PIP auto payer not paying your full, billed amount, it is appropriate to ask the patient to pay any balance due.

Corrective billing

If a claim you have submitted is rejected due to missing or incorrect information, then you will need to re-submit the claim after making any necessary changes to bring it into compliance with the payer's information system. This is called "corrective billing". Examples of this could include an incorrect or missing date of birth or member identification number, the wrong health plan name, no authorization or claim number, non-specific diagnosis code or CPT codes that are not in your contract or outside of your scope of practice. In other cases the plan may dispute the medical necessity of the services billed for and deny payment. In some cases certain plans may determine a service to be experimental in nature where another plan might cover it without a question. In any case, you need to go to bat for yourself and re-submit the claim.

When submitting corrective billing, in addition to making any changes on the claim form, you may also need to enclose chart notes for the date of service in question. You may also need to send in a short explanation of why the service provided was medically necessary, or explain why the service should be covered under your state's law. On the top of the claim form you may handwrite "corrective billing" and "supporting documents attached". Highlight it as well as any changes made to the claim and hope for the best. As always, if the insurance payer declines to provide reimbursement for the services you may bill the patient directly unless prohibited under terms of your contract with the payer.

PIP auto insurance

Billing for reimbursement under the personal injury protection (PIP) benefits of a patient's automobile insurance plan for injuries sustained during an automobile accident can often be a frustrating experience. Taking the time to understand a few important points, however, can ease many potential difficulties. First, understand that even if the other driver's insurance is ultimately responsible, it is the patient's own plan that should be billed by you.

A patient's PIP plan will pay for their own medical care in order to avoid any delay in the patient getting care should the other party's plan balk at making payment. Later on, when the case is settled, the at-fault party's plan will make a payment to the patient's plan to reimburse them for any payments made on the patient's behalf up to the limits of their policy.

You should verify benefits for the patient's PIP insurance just as you would for any other payer. In addition to the questions on your regular checklist, ask the adjuster assigned to the claim if the claim is still open and if there are any PIP benefits remaining.

If the accident was two years ago and the patient saw a chiropractor the entire time then chances are good there are few, if any, funds left for additional medical coverage. My first PIP claim came back with a check for 79¢ and a note saying that this was all that was left of the patient's $10,000 PIP benefit. I promptly went out and raised my own policy's limit to $35,000 to avoid a similar situation.

If you are in a state where your practitioner type requires a referral from an MD prior to treatment, be sure to obtain this and send a copy with every claim form. Also be sure to obtain the correct claim number, and if required by the plan, authorization number. It is a good idea to speak with the claims adjuster prior to submitting any claims to find out if there are any potential problems that can be avoided ahead of time, rather than waiting several months only to discover they will not pay your claims.

Most claims adjusters will insist on reviewing your chart notes prior to making any payment. You can submit your claim and then wait for them to ask you for the chart notes, thereby allowing you to charge them an extra fee for this service (for which they are legally obligated to pay under most states' laws). Doing this, however, can mean the addition of a few months to the payment cycle, as they will usually wait for you to call them when you finally remember that the claim hasn't been paid. Then they will tell you they need chart notes and take another month or two before finally issuing a check.

Keep it simple and just send the chart notes for every date of service on the claim form each time you submit one. You will quickly come to appreciate the difference in your cash flow. Of course, you must have proper permission from the patient to share this information. HIPAA prevents you from supplying information which was not specifically requested, so get a note faxed to you from the adjuster saying that they will require chart notes before you just start sending them in.

PIP claims adjusters are notorious for attempting to discourage practitioners from charging their full usual & customary charges, as well as denying payments based upon nonsensical reasoning and in some cases actually threatening practitioners with an investigation of insurance fraud in order to intimidate the practitioner into reducing their billed charges. It pays to know what your state's laws are regarding PIP medical payment so that you can quote relevant passages as needed. This drives adjusters crazy! This information can be obtained from your state's office of the insurance commissioner or any good PIP lawyer.

If necessary, don't hesitate to file a complaint with your state's office of the insurance commissioner. Four times out of five filing an official complaint and standing up to an ornery adjuster results in immediate payment. Know your rights and don't be afraid to fight for what is right. You will be helping to change their perception of CAM providers as being uninformed and easily manipulated.

Again, as with any insurance scenario, if the PIP insurer does not pay your full, billed amount you may bill the patient directly for the remaining balance, or submit a secondary claim to the patient's health insurance plan. When coordinating benefits between a PIP payer and the patient's health insurance plan, one large health insurer suggests that you send claims to both the PIP payer and the health insurance payer at the same time so that when the PIP benefits are exhausted both parties will have records of the claims (for when the health insurance payer begins its investigation). This also will prevent any issues concerning untimely filing for the secondary payer.

Third-party payers

If the patient's PIP benefits have been exhausted or they don't have any insurance coverage, they may ask you to wait for payment from the third party's insurance company. This is up to you whether or not you want to do this. Most states allow up to three years from the date of the accident for the parties to reach a settlement, so any payments made for your services may not be received by you for quite a while. If you aren't that busy and have the time, why not go ahead and treat the patient? You'll hopefully be looking at a nice, fat check at some unknown point down the road. Remember, though, that it can be increasingly difficult to actually collect the full balance due as more time goes by. Patients move, attorneys change offices and paperwork gets lost.

If you do accept patients with third-party payers, always file a lien at your county court house against the patient in order to protect your interest in the eventual settlement. Even this does not guarantee payment, but it will give you legal documentation to reference when the eventual settlement occurs.

Contact a PIP attorney in your area and ask them to send you a blank lien form that meets the local formatting requirements for your county. Most of them need to have specific margin sizes and may have other requirements. You will need to have the form notarized at the courthouse and they will send a copy to the patient. Advise your patient that this is standard procedure with this type of case so as not to alarm them. It is advised that you re-file a lien at least once per year to keep your name fresh in the patient's mind and in their attorney's file.

Also, have both the patient and their attorney sign a form stating that they will protect your interests and make full payment to you from the settlement funds before any money goes to the patient. This is somewhat less effective than filing a lien but the redundancy won't hurt anything.

Establishing a relationship with a good PIP attorney near you can be helpful as they can provide you with advice and forms that are standard for your county.

Denials

Opening up an envelope from an insurance company only to find there is no check enclosed can be disheartening. Unfortunately, denials are more common than should be acceptable but they are just another part of the insurance billing landscape. The denial of a claim can occur for many different reasons. In most cases there is a relatively simple solution. In some cases, though, it will feel like you hit a wall and can't go anywhere. Approach a denial the same way you would a patient. The first step is to diagnose the problem and then identify the appropriate remedy.

The first place to look for clues is on the explanation of benefits form (EOB). There will usually be either an explanation of why the claim was not paid or a message code for each denied service. Message codes often can be correlated to an answer key that is on the back of the EOB or at the bottom of the page. In the case of some companies with a penchant for complexity you may need to reference their website for a complete list of their message codes. In any case, you can always call the company and ask for more detailed information.

Before assuming there was an outright denial made, be sure to check that the amount that should have been paid wasn't credited toward the patient's deductible. Sometimes this isn't clear and requires a second look. If it was applied to the deductible, then the claim wasn't denied- you will just need to bill the amount to the patient, as they are responsible for paying this amount, not the insurance payer.

In many cases, the claim is denied because there was a misunderstanding or omission of information at the time you verified benefits. If the insurance payer only covers your type of service with a referral but you didn't ask if a referral was required, then you are reaping the harvest of your own lack of detail. It is an all too frequent occurrence that a denied claim could have been avoided by being more thorough during the benefits verification. Unfortunately this lesson needs to be learned several times by most practitioners. If it is a simple matter of having submitted an incorrect code or the wrong date of birth, etc, then you can make the necessary changes and resubmit the claim as corrective billing.

Sometimes a family member with the same name will be denied as a duplicate claim. Be sure the date of birth is correct and, if applicable, there is a distinguishing field identifying that family member. If a denial occurs for this reason, call and ask for the information to be corrected.

If a claim appears to be in a perpetually pending state it may be that the payer has sent an "incident report" to the patient to fill out and return before the claim can be paid. This type of form typically verifies whether the diagnosis being treated was the result of a work or auto-related accident or injury. It also is used to ascertain if the treatment was primarily for wellness care or a preexisting condition. Patients can be intimidated by these forms and "lose" them frequently, thus putting your claims in a state of stasis.

You can request blank copies of these forms yourself from the payer and give them to the patient to fill out at your office, or even have the patient call the payer from your office and give the information verbally over the phone in many cases. If the member states that they have submitted the form the provider must wait a required time frame before billing the member. Usually there will be a message code on an EOB indicating patient's responsibility once the plan has made its determination.

In many cases the claim was denied because of an error on the part of the insurance payer. This can be as simple as "we can't find your claim in the system" or as complex as "all claims for the past 6 months are stuck in the imaging department's scanning software and we have a team working on it". In some cases you will get a response such as "oh, yeah, that doesn't look right, let me fix that for you". What it comes down to is this- if you don't call and inquire as to the reason for the denial then you won't know how to begin resolving the problem. It takes time, but it is a necessary evil so make peace with it, make a cup of tea, and get a speakerphone for when you are on hold.

The main thing to remember regarding denied claims is that you will need to put in some elbow grease to resolve the situation. They don't fix themselves. The longer you ignore them, the harder they are to figure out. The more you have to figure out, the more intimidating it feels, the more likely you are to procrastinate, and the more likely it becomes that you will not get paid for those dates of service. Do you like working for free? No one does. It is not enough to provide your service. To quote an anonymous small business owner "you need to eat your kill".

On the other hand, if you find that you are spending an inordinate amount of time and energy troubleshooting one company's claims then that is good information. Perhaps you would be better off not billing claims to that particular company. Remember that time spent on paperwork reduces the time you can be spending face to face with your patients and that is where your income is generated.

Appeals & complaints

If you find yourself in a situation where you think you are right and the claims representative isn't budging then it is time to avail yourself of the plan's appeals process. The patient must usually initiate the appeals process by sending a letter to the payer. Included with this letter is any supporting documentation necessary, which you may need to provide.

The insurance plan will usually respond within 30 days to an appeal. If you and your patient decide to go this route, keep in mind that the appeal needs to be submitted in a timely fashion to have any impact. If you are filing an appeal well after the denial occurred and too much time has gone by then you might as well not bother. Appeals do get results in some cases so it is worth doing and just like anything else- if it's worth doing, do it well.

If your claim still isn't paid after all attempts to fix the problem you should bill the patient, if you haven't already. Remember, the patient is ultimately responsible for the payment of their care. Hopefully you had them sign a financial agreement to this effect. If you still believe you are right and that the claim was wrongly denied then you should file a complaint with your state's office of the insurance commissioner. Many states have an easy, online form that takes just a few minutes to fill out over the internet. These complaints can sometimes get results when all other attempts to resolve a problem failed. If nothing else, complaints will reflect a pattern of problems with a specific insurance company over time and can be useful when consumers are researching plans. It only takes a few complaints to get the attention of powerful players in the marketplace.

Collecting patient payments

Unless a patient's insurance plan covers 100% of the reimbursement rate there is a portion left over that is the patient's responsibility. If there is a fixed-dollar amount in the form of a co-pay, then this should be collected at the time of service. If there is a co-insurance percentage, then this is usually collected after the fact, as is any amount applied toward satisfying the deductible.

Collecting payment from your patients is just as important as collecting payment from the insurance payers. In many cases the patient owes more than their insurance company does and if you are lax in attempting to collect this then you could potentially lose out on being paid fairly for your hard work.

If a patient says they don't have their checkbook with them when you ask for their co-pay then let them know that you accept Visa & MasterCard. Most people carry a debit or credit card with them and if you make this form of payment available to them you will collect payment much more efficiently. After the initial expense of purchasing the credit card machine (never rent or lease one- it is very expensive) your monthly expenses will be minimal. The small percentage you pay for charging cards is outweighed by the increased cash flow as the charged amount is deposited directly into your checking account within 24 hours. Card processing fees may total $500-1,000 or so for an entire year, but in many cases much more than that goes uncollected when patients are allowed to leave the office without making payment.

Trying to collect the co-pay after the patient has left is twice as difficult as just asking for it at the time of service. Most patients with a co-pay as part of their plan have a contractual obligation to pay you at the time the service is rendered. If you are a contracted provider with their plan then you also have a legal obligation to collect the co-pay. Psychologically, once a patient has left the office they are more likely to forget and to procrastinate making payment when reminded. Do yourself a favor and do it right the first time. Get in the habit of collecting all co-pays when the patient first enters your office.

Co-insurance amounts are different, as in many cases you won't know the exact dollar amount of the patient's portion until you receive the EOB. Plans with a deductible also work this way. If the deductible hasn't been met for the year, then you will have to wait and see how much of the reimbursement amount will be applied toward satisfying the deductible.

If you have not collected payment at the time of service, you will receive the EOB and see exactly how much the patient owes you. This is the time to send the patient a statement asking for payment. Do not wait too long to send out patient statements as the balances owing may grow too large and psychologically it becomes more difficult for the patient to make payment. Frequently, patients are intimidated by receiving bills. Send your statements frequently so that your patients can't forget you, and also to keep the balance due in a comfortable range. Don't wait until your patient owes you $500 before sending a bill!

One exception to waiting for the EOB before billing the co-insurance amount to the patient is when you are an out-of-network, non-contracted provider. In this case, you know exactly what the patient will owe based upon the percentage the insurance plan covers for your services. If the plan covers out-of-network practitioners at 70% then the patient will owe you 30% of your billed charges. If the plan covers 50% then the patient will owe you 50%. This you should collect at the time of service. It gets difficult when you are in-network and the contracted reimbursement rates are discounted from your billed rates and you are also billing multiple codes. In this case it is much simpler to wait and let the EOB tell you how much the patient owes, unless you keep excellent records on each plan's fee schedule and can calculate the patient portion confidently.

If you are a non-contracted practitioner and are considered out-of-network, then you may consider telling the patient that when you file the claim it is at 100% of your billed rates, so their balance due will be higher than if they just paid you in full at the time of service at your time of service, discount rate. In this case the patient would send in your superbill and wait for reimbursement. Ultimately they will receive a payment and their out-of-pocket total will be less than if you billed for them because the percentages are based upon the prompt-payment-discount rate, not the full, billed rate. This will reduce the total amount paid by your patient in the long term and also increases your cash flow and eliminates your time spent managing the claim.

If you are working on an insurance claim that is taking much longer than normal to get paid, stay in communication with the patient to let them know it is still in process. This way when you finally do send them a statement for their portion you are fresher in their mind. People resent being billed for something that happened a year or more ago after not having heard anything from the provider the entire time. They assume the claim was paid or the balance written off. Then, when they receive a bill for a large dollar amount with no warning it can be upsetting. Send statements, or at least a note, updating them on their account status regularly.

If a patient does run up a large balance (anything in excess of $200) call them to discuss making payment over the phone with a credit card. Offer a payment plan if necessary, but have them commit to paying something right then. If they accept a payment plan, do not take more than 90 days to pay down the balance in full. The debt becomes much more difficult to collect if the process continues for greater than three months. Be sure to send them a statement every month showing them what they agreed to and what the payment amount due is.

Make it as easy as possible to for patients to pay you. Processing credit & debit cards will go a long way toward helping your cash flow. When you don't collect up-front, be sure to send out patient statements regularly. Always include a pre-addressed return envelope with each statement you mail out. Writing a hand-written, personalized note on the statement explaining why the balance is due can be effective as many patients are confused by their insurance to begin with. Use a yellow highlighter pen to highlight the amount due. Make your statements easy to read. Keep things visually simple to look at.

If a patient does not pay in response to a statement you sent, then send another one within 4 weeks. Follow up with a personal phone call if you still don't receive payment. Maybe they were just out of town on a long vacation, or maybe they lost their job and can't pay the entire amount. Either way, you won't know if you don't check in with them. Don't let them forget you!

Be sure to review an accounts receivable (A/R) aging report every two weeks to keep track of who isn't paying you in a timely fashion. It is easy to let time lapse when you are busy in your practice but setting aside the time to stay abreast of your A/R will help to keep the money in your cash flow pipeline flowing toward you.

In extreme cases of non-payment you may consider using a collections agency but these services can charge up to 50% of the amount collected and can generate ill will depending upon their collections tactics. Sometimes just threatening to list the amount owing as a bad debt on the patient's credit report will stimulate action on their part. Don't plan on having this patient schedule any future appointments or refer family members, but if they are disrespecting you by not honoring your financial agreement then you are probably better off without them.

It is up to you how far to go with your attempts to collect. If the amount is less than a couple of hundred dollars then perhaps it is better to chalk it up as a learning experience and trust that the patient's karma will bring them their own life lessons. When a debt goes bad and is un-collectable be sure to review what happened and what you can do different the next time that a similar situation arises.

If you see a pattern of similar situations occurring then you need to evaluate your system and find out where it is breaking down. Perhaps your policies need revising, or you need to communicate better what the patient's responsibilities are before you begin providing services. Learn from your mistakes and then move on. The bottom line is to maintain a clear system for tracking payments and make it easy for your patients to pay you.

Billing software

If you are only sending in a few claims every now and then you probably can keep track of things with a simple ledger system. However, if you are submitting more than a few claims each week then you should probably look into using some billing software.

There are several very affordable programs available and more are being introduced every year as software developers recognize this fast-growing market. Using a software program to track your claims can be quite easy and the time saved will quickly pay for the cost of the software. A good program can help you keep track of many more details than a paper system, as well as allowing you instant access to reports showing late claims that are aging beyond a reasonable time period.

There are some programs, such as Just Claims, which does what the name implies and only generate properly formatted claim forms with no extra bells and whistles. For those who need some method of tracking aged claims and performing basic accounts receivables management, a program such as HikfaMaster will perform well and give you basic reporting capabilities as well as the ability to manage patient information and generate mailing labels for your patients and referring physicians. HikfaMaster also integrates electronic claims submission, email & birthday lists and inventory tracking.

Programs such as Client Tracker take it a step further and integrate SOAP note charting and appointment scheduling. A similar program is Acubase, which adds the extra feature of a reference database of Chinese herbs and acupuncture points.

For those with more advanced reporting needs and who want to use an industry-standard program for future data portability considerations, Medisoft does a good job, yet involves a steeper learning curve for the novice user. Medisoft and comparable programs can also provide custom practice analysis reports to help you stay on top of trends in your practice.

If you plan on outsourcing your billing to an independent service at some point in the future, you should consider which programs are most widely used in your area before buying one. It will be important to have a program that will allow easy data transfer to the program a billing service uses. One of the most widely used programs for smaller billing services with smaller clients, such as CAM providers, is Medisoft. Call around and find out what programs other providers are using and how satisfied they are with their software. Most programs create updated versions each year so you may also want to contact various vendors and find out what upcoming changes are expected in their software.

Detailed information about most programs can be found on the web and many of them have screen shots and virtual tours of the software online. In some cases you may also be able to download a demo copy of the software to try out before buying. Compare a few programs to see how easy it is to navigate through the various screens as well as how intuitive the functions are. Some programs give you a headache just to look at them, with poorly designed screens and complicated navigational structures with non-standard names for basic functions. Make sure you choose one that matches your own level of computer skill and won't take forever to learn how to use. You are a CAM provider, not a computer geek. Choose a program that will allow you to focus on patient care, not keeping you on the phone to tech-support every other day.

Electronic claims submission

Electronic billing is a function that is becoming more standard in most software programs. This function allows a user to submit claims electronically to the insurance payer over a secure internet system via a middleman insurance claims clearinghouse. To use this feature you must establish an account with a clearinghouse, procure identification numbers from each insurance payer you will be submitting to and have your software configured correctly to interface with the clearinghouse.

Submitting claims electronically often will shorten the reimbursement cycle to as little as two weeks for clean claims. You instantly receive an electronic receipt of the claim having been delivered so there can be no excuse that "we never received your claim". Electronic billing eliminates the extra paper and postage and errors in handling the paper claims. It is not free, but for a busy office with a lot of insurance business, it can make quite a difference.

While some larger payers will have their own free electronic submissions systems in place for contracted providers, most practitioners turn to a clearinghouse that can process claims for multiple payers and which in turn charges a small fee per claim for the service. This new service has quickly become a multi-billion dollar per year industry with some major players positioning themselves for the long haul with a wide variety of value-added services. The average practitioner, however, won't need the extra bells and whistles and can look for less-expensive, stripped-down versions.

One of the biggest and best clearinghouses providing national coverage is NDCHealth. This service will even process your claims for payers who do not yet accept electronic claims and stuff the envelope for you, saving you a trip to the post office. Another service that some providers have had good experiences with is eClaims.

For most clearinghouses there is a per-claim fee of about 40-50 cents. Some local payers, such as Washington State's Regence, provide electronic billing and clearinghouse services for free to contracted providers.

Remember, every chance you have, you need to jump on opportunities to improve your cash flow and reduce the turn-around time for your claims. The monthly charges for using an electronic claims clearinghouse may look like an unwanted addition to your overhead, but the cost will quickly justify itself through increased cash flow and fewer rejected claims.

Once the system is set up it actually takes less time because you don't have to stuff the envelopes and you can batch process many claims at once. New clearinghouses are appearing on the scene all the time, so ask around at the billing offices of local doctor's offices and find out which clearinghouse they are using and if they are happy with the service.

Billing services

If you do not have the type of constitution that tolerates the extra time in front of the computer doing billing-related tasks, then you should consider out-sourcing your claims processing to a reputable billing service. There are many, many services doing business in almost every town, so carefully choosing the right one for your practice is extremely important. Using a good billing service will save you 4-6 hours per week that you can instead spend with your patients generating more income. Using a poor billing service will cost you innumerable hours later on deciphering mountains of un-reconciled information and suffering through long dry spells with little cash flow.

Always check references for any company or individual you are considering contracting to do this work for you. Find out how long they have been in business. Do they have experience billing for your provider type? Billing for acupuncture is very different than billing for massage therapy and billing for naturopathic medicine services is much more complicated than either acupuncture or massage. Don't volunteer to be a guinea pig for an inexperienced biller.

Find out what software they are using and how portable the data is in the event you need to change to another billing service. Do they process claims electronically? What do their aging reports look like- are they easy to read or mysterious and difficult to translate into lay-terms? Do they back-up the data off-site regularly? Will they send you a weekly backup of your files? These are some important questions to ask before diving into a contractual relationship. You also need to define exactly what they will and will not do for you. Will they call and verify the benefits for each new patient or is that your responsibility?

There is nothing worse than finding out three months later that no benefits have been verified the entire time because each of you thought the other was doing that. Does their fee include postage and supplies or is that extra? What provisions are in place when the billing person goes on vacation or falls ill? Will they do the follow-up work to get late claims paid? Do they send out patient statements or is that your job? How many other clients do they have?

Most billing services charge a fee per claim. This can be either a flat fee for every claim submitted or a percentage of the amount actually collected. Obviously there is more of an incentive for the billing service to do the work necessary to actually collect each claim if they don't get paid until you do. This also is the more expensive option. Standard fees can range from $2 per claim, or 5-10% of the total collected dollar amount. Some individuals performing billing services prefer to be paid by the hour for time spent managing your claims. If it is a reputable person that has excellent references and a solid history this can work out well. Reasonable hourly rates for an experienced biller can be around $18-22.

When outsourcing to a billing service you just send them your day sheets and copies of new patient information and insurance cards as well as EOB's and a record of patient payments that you have received. Make sure this happens at least at weekly intervals and that the claims are sent out at least once a week. Verify that the billing service is HIPAA compliant in order to insure your own compliance and to fully protect patient information.

For those who run a very busy practice and have a receptionist or other office staff you can teach them to do your billing for you and keep the tasks in-house. It is best to have one person designated to perform these tasks or to oversee that the tasks are executed efficiently and in a timely fashion.

End note

Take the time to research your options and follow the business model that is most appropriate for you as an individual. Billing can be weirdly satisfying when you have a solid system humming along efficiently. Whether you do the tasks yourself or delegate them to a third party it is nice to know that you are helping your patients get good healthcare and that is what ultimately makes it all worth it.

If you have comments or questions as you begin applying this information to your practice please visit our website where we will continue to post updated information as it becomes available. We're also interested in your feedback so we can improve future revisions of this book.

You may be eligible for CE credits for having read this book. Check in at our website for more information.

Finally, an optional, companion CDrom is available with customizable billing forms and templates for you to reference.

Visit us at:

www.SamsaraPublishing.com

Resources

Additional insurance billing info:

www.SamsaraPublishing.com

Billing Software:

www.DemberDatabaseDesign.com

www.GingkoSoftware.com

www.Trigram.com

www.Medisoft.com

Electronic Billing Clearinghouses:

www.NDCHealth.com

www.eClaims.com

Custom Printed Supplies, Bulk CMS 1500 Forms:

www.MedicalArtsPress.com

HikfaMaster

Insurance-Billing Software for Independent Health-Care Practices

- Extremely easy to learn and use.
- Automatically fills in your bills based on stored practice information.
- Calibrated HCFA/CMS-1500 printing.
- Electronic billing.
- Accounts Receivable with payment tracking and flexible report/statement generator.
- Good for health insurance, auto insurance and self-paying patients.
- E-mail, mailing labels, birthday finder.
- Windows and Macintosh
- Comes with printed user manual.
- Free technical support.

For More Information Contact Dember Database Design:

info@demberdatabase.com

www.demberdatabase.com/hikfamaster